FASCINATING
FOOD
CHAINS

Decomposers

Megan Lappi

MEDIA ENHANCED BOOKS
AV2
BY WEIGL
ADDED VALUE • AUDIO VISUAL

www.av2books.com

MEDIA ENHANCED BOOKS
AV² BY WEIGL™
ADDED VALUE • AUDIO VISUAL

AV² provides enriched content that supplements and complements this book. Weigl's AV² books strive to create inspired learning and engage young minds in a total learning experience.

Your AV² Media Enhanced books come alive with...

Audio
Listen to sections of the book read aloud.

Key Words
Study vocabulary, and complete a matching word activity.

Video
Watch informative video clips.

Quizzes
Test your knowledge.

Embedded Weblinks
Gain additional information for research.

Slide Show
View images and captions, and prepare a presentation.

Try This!
Complete activities and hands-on experiments.

... and much, much more!

Go to www.av2books.com, and enter this book's unique code.

BOOK CODE
S 5 6 7 4 9 6

AV² by Weigl brings you media enhanced books that support active learning.

Published by AV² by Weigl
350 5th Avenue, 59th Floor
New York, NY 10118
Website: www.av2books.com

Library of Congress Cataloging-in-Publication Data

Names: Lappi, Megan, author.
Title: Decomposers / Megan Lappi.
Description: New York, NY : AV2 by Weigl, 2017. | Series: Fascinating food chains | Includes index.
Identifiers: LCCN 2016051919 (print) | LCCN 2016052301 (ebook) | ISBN 9781489657763 (hard cover : alk. paper) | ISBN 9781489657770 (soft cover : alk. paper) | ISBN 9781489657787 (multi-user ebk.)
Subjects: LCSH: Biodegradation--Juvenile literature.
Classification: LCC QH530.5 .L37 2017 (print) | LCC QH530.5 (ebook) | DDC 581.7/14--dc23
LC record available at https://lccn.loc.gov/2016051919

Printed in the United States of America in Brainerd, Minnesota
1 2 3 4 5 6 7 8 9 0   21 20 19 18 17

022017
310117

Project Coordinator: John Willis   Designer: Ana Maria Vidal

Every reasonable effort has been made to trace ownership and to obtain permission to reprint copyright material. The publisher would be pleased to have any errors or omissions brought to its attention so that they may be corrected in subsequent printings.

The publisher acknowledges Getty Images, iStock, Shutterstock, Minden Pictures, Dreamstime, and Alamy as its primary image suppliers for this title.

CONTENTS

2 AV² Book Code

4 What Is a Food Chain?

6 Decomposers

8 The Bottom of the Food Chain

10 Tiny Decomposers

12 Types of Fungi

14 Unique Decomposers

16 Decomposers around the World

18 Nature's Recyclers

20 Energy Pyramids

22 Quiz

23 Key Words/Index

24 Log on to www.av2books.com

What Is a Food Chain?

All living things need food to survive. Food provides the **energy** that plants and animals need to grow and thrive. Plants and animals do not rely on the same types of food to live. Plants make their own food. They use energy from the Sun and water from the soil. Some animals eat plants. Others eat animals that have eaten plants. In this way, all living things are connected to each other. These connections form food chains.

A food chain is made up of **producers** and **consumers**. All of the world's organisms belong to one of these groups. Plants are the main producers in a food chain. This is because they make energy that can be used by the rest of the living things on Earth.

Consumers are living things that receive their energy from producers. There are five types of consumers in a food chain. They are carnivores, decomposers, herbivores, omnivores, and parasites.

There are thousands of types of molds. Mold grows best in places where the air is warm and wet.

Food Chain

SUN

DECOMPOSER

Producer
Consumers
Sun

CARNIVORE

OMNIVORE

PARASITE

Parasites can feed
from living things
found at all levels
of a food chain.

HERBIVORE

PRODUCER

Decomposers

Decomposers are a key part of the food chain. They are living things that get their energy by eating and breaking down dead plants and animals. It takes many decomposers to break down decaying **matter**.

Decomposers help keep an **ecosystem** clean by clearing away the material left behind by plants and animals that have died. This material is called detritus. Decomposers are part of the detritus food chain. Some of the most important types of decomposers are very small. Bacteria have just one cell, the smallest unit that living things are made of. Fungi are decomposers that use special cells called spores to reproduce, or create new fungi.

Detritivores are a special type of decomposer. They are animals that break down plants and animals by eating dead material. Detritivores include earthworms, maggots, and termites.

Other decomposers break down dead plants and animals using **enzymes**. Many of the **nutrients** from this process pass into the soil. Other nutrients enter bodies of water.

A woodlouse uses its senses of smell and taste to find food. Much of its food comes from dead plants.

Shelf fungi grow on both living and dead trees. They get their food from the body of the tree.

About **100,000** bacteria can be found on **0.2 square inches** (1.3 square centimeters) of human skin.

Maggots live for **eight to ten** days, and then change to another form.

Earthworms range in length from **1 inch** (2.5 cm) to **12 feet** (3.7 meters).

There are about **99,000** known types of fungi.

The Bottom of the Food Chain

Detritivores and other decomposers are at the bottom of the food chain. They are very important because the nutrients they produce are needed by plants in order to grow. Without decomposers, herbivores, or animals that rely on plants for food energy, would not have plants to eat.

The process of breaking down matter begins with a detritivore, such as an earthworm. Earthworms break down detritus into smaller pieces. This gives the earthworm the energy and nutrients it needs.

Then, tiny decomposers, such as bacteria, complete the process. They release a number of chemicals that break down the pieces of detritus. This makes the pieces even smaller. Soil and water are able to absorb, or take in, these small pieces. The cycle is repeated after this.

Although some millipedes will feed on fresh vegetation, most eat dead or decaying plants.

Parts of the Chain

The detritus food chain is made up of the following parts:

detritus + detritivores + decomposers = nutrients for air, soil, and water

Tiny Decomposers

Bacteria are everywhere. They live in the air, in water, and on the ground. Bacteria are so tiny that millions of them could live in a space as small as the end of a pencil.

Scientists once believed bacteria were animals because they moved around. However, scientists later realized that bacteria are not animals. Then, they wondered if bacteria could be plants. Now, scientists know that bacteria are neither plants nor animals. They are a separate form of life.

Bacteria make up the biggest group of decomposers. If bacteria did not exist, dead matter and waste would pile up. The nutrients contained in the dead matter and waste would be lost.

Bacteria living in the ground break down dead plants and animals into nutrients. In this way, bacteria add nutrients to the soil. The roots of plants growing in the soil take up the nutrients, helping the plants to grow.

Bacteria are important decomposers. However, some can cause diseases, making them harmful to animals.

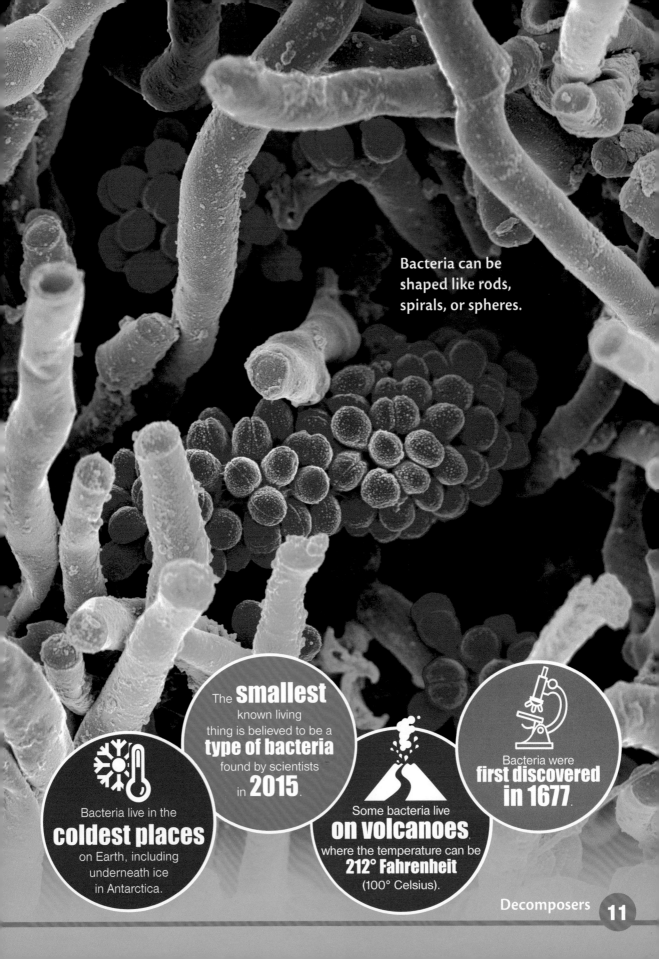

Bacteria can be shaped like rods, spirals, or spheres.

Bacteria live in the **coldest places** on Earth, including underneath ice in Antarctica.

The **smallest** known living thing is believed to be a **type of bacteria** found by scientists in **2015**.

Some bacteria live **on volcanoes**, where the temperature can be **212° Fahrenheit** (100° Celsius).

Bacteria were **first discovered in 1677**.

Types of Fungi

There are many different types of fungi. Some are very small. Others can grow as large as a dog. Examples of fungi are mushrooms, mold, and mildew. Fungi act in a similar way to bacteria. They produce chemicals that break down material in their **habitat**.

Most fungi are not harmful, but a few can cause severe illness if eaten. Dangerous fungi include white destroying angel mushrooms and death cap mushrooms. They are part of a group of mushrooms known as the amanita family. Other members of the amanita family are safe to eat.

Some fungi are named after the foods they look like. For example, the chicken of the woods mushroom looks similar to a large, yellow chicken. In Germany, people like to eat this fungus. Cooked chicken of the woods mushrooms tastes much like chicken.

Veiled lady mushrooms have been used as medicine for about 1,400 years.

Powdery mildew grows on plants.
It can be found in places where
days are warm and nights are cool.

Some mushrooms are **fully grown** less than a day after they emerge from the ground.

Until **1969**, scientists thought that fungi were plants.

A single **honey mushroom**, which covers 3.4 square miles (8.8 square kilometers) in Oregon, is thought to be **2,400** years old.

A spoonful of **garden soil** may contain **1 million** fungi.

Unique Decomposers

There are many kinds of decomposers. Some, such as bacteria, are too small to be seen by the human eye. Detritivores such as earthworms and millipedes are large enough for human eyes to see without a **microscope**. Decomposers can be found throughout the world. Some decomposers live in water. Many live on land.

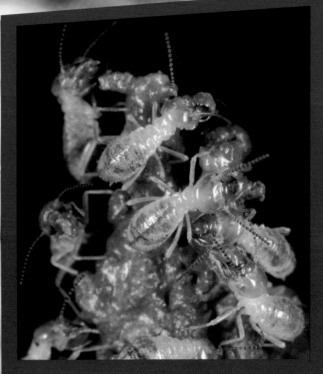

Termites

- Feed on both living and dead trees and other plants

- About 2,300 **species** exist

- May cause severe damage to buildings and objects made of wood

Maggots

- Larvae, or young form, of the common housefly

- Breathe using two small holes at their back end

- Used in medical treatment to clean dead cells from wounds

Ascomycetes

- Make up the largest group of fungi

- Found on dead animals, in fresh water, and in soil

- Used to make the **antibiotic** penicillin, a medicine to treat infections

Earthworms

- Consist of more than 1,800 species

- Have both male and female parts

- Make tunnels in the soil that create space in which air and water can move around

Molds

- Are a tiny type of fungi

- Cause food to spoil

- Are used to make some cheeses and certain vitamins

Decomposers around the World

Look at the map to see where some types of decomposers may live. Can you think of other decomposers? Where on the map do they live?

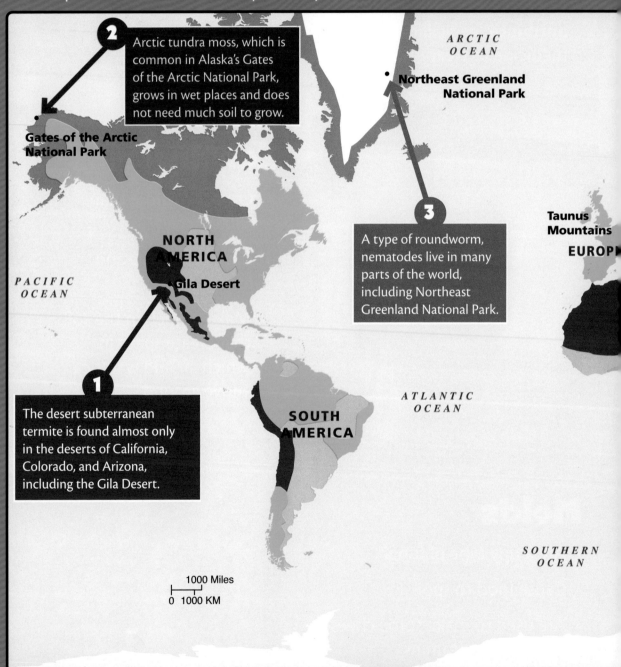

2 Arctic tundra moss, which is common in Alaska's Gates of the Arctic National Park, grows in wet places and does not need much soil to grow.

Gates of the Arctic National Park

ARCTIC OCEAN

• **Northeast Greenland National Park**

3 A type of roundworm, nematodes live in many parts of the world, including Northeast Greenland National Park.

Taunus Mountains

EUROPE

NORTH AMERICA

• **Gila Desert**

PACIFIC OCEAN

1 The desert subterranean termite is found almost only in the deserts of California, Colorado, and Arizona, including the Gila Desert.

SOUTH AMERICA

ATLANTIC OCEAN

SOUTHERN OCEAN

1000 Miles
0 1000 KM

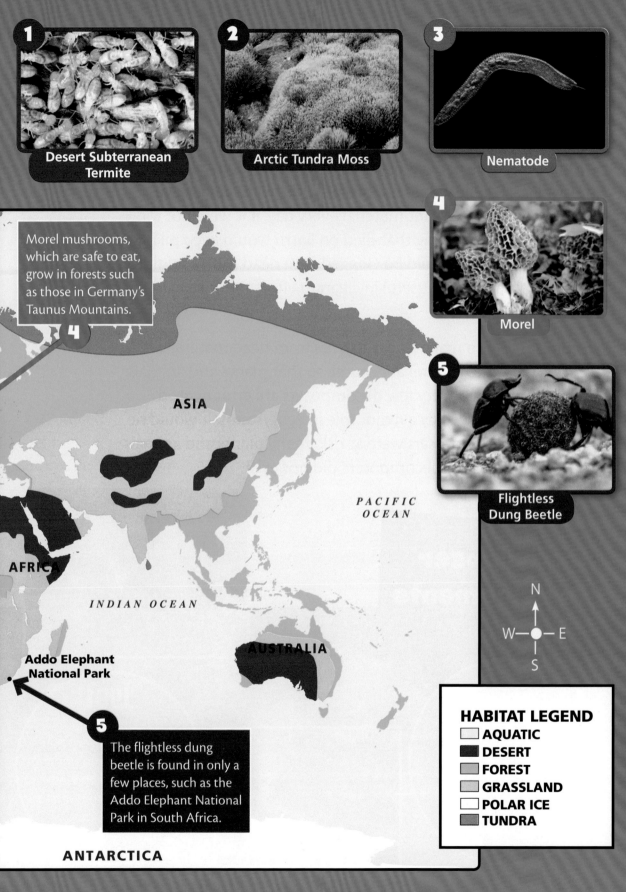

1 Desert Subterranean Termite

2 Arctic Tundra Moss

3 Nematode

4 Morel mushrooms, which are safe to eat, grow in forests such as those in Germany's Taunus Mountains.

4 Morel

ASIA

PACIFIC OCEAN

5 Flightless Dung Beetle

AFRICA

INDIAN OCEAN

AUSTRALIA

Addo Elephant National Park

N
W — E
S

5 The flightless dung beetle is found in only a few places, such as the Addo Elephant National Park in South Africa.

ANTARCTICA

HABITAT LEGEND
AQUATIC
DESERT
FOREST
GRASSLAND
POLAR ICE
TUNDRA

Nature's Recyclers

Without the work of decomposers, the world would be a messy place. People would have to walk through fallen leaves, logs, and other dead plant material every day. If it were not for decomposers, everything that died on Earth would keep piling up. Lakes and rivers would be clogged with dead fish. In addition, some decomposers are useful in cleanup efforts after certain types of accidents.

Decomposers also make sure nutrients from dead material are recycled back into the soil and water, so that plants and animals can use them again. Very few decomposers are **endangered**. However, since they play a major role in ecosystems, it would be important if decomposers were at risk. Many plants and animals would be in danger if decomposers did not exist.

Decomposer Developments

1989
Bacteria are used to help clean beaches in Alaska after the tanker *Exxon Valdez* strikes a reef, spilling huge amounts of oil.

1991
The United States issues a recovery plan for the American burying beetle, which was once common but had become rare by the 1980s.

In The Field
Microbiologist

Microbiologists are scientists who study organisms, or living things, that are too small to see. These organisms include bacteria and some types of fungi.

Education Most microbiologists receive at least a bachelor's degree in chemistry or biology. For some jobs, a master's or doctorate degree is needed.

Working Conditions Some microbiologists make sure that food is safe to eat. Others work in the field, studying how bacteria and fungi affect the environment. Some microbiologists perform research in laboratories.

Tools

- Field Equipment: Collection bottles and jars, tweezers, gloves
- Lab Equipment: Microscope, computer, test tubes, beakers

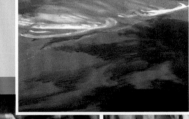

2006
The International Union for Conservation of Nature lists the Badplaas black millipede, which is found only in South Africa, as endangered.

2016
Scientists discover that communities of natural bacteria can work together to help clean up oil spills.

Energy Pyramids

A food chain is one way to chart the transfer of energy from one living thing to another. Another way to show how living things are connected is through an energy pyramid. An energy pyramid starts with the Sun. The Sun provides the energy that allows producers to grow. Producers are a source of energy for primary consumers in the next level of the pyramid. Primary consumers transfer energy up the pyramid to tertiary consumers. In this way, all living things depend on one another for survival. In the example below, grass is food for deer, and deer are food for jaguars.

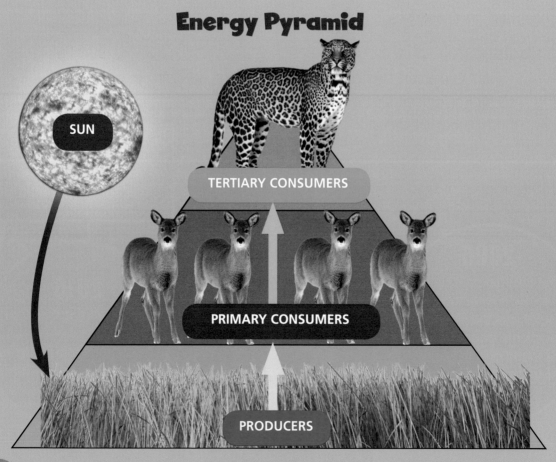

Energy Pyramid

SUN

TERTIARY CONSUMERS

PRIMARY CONSUMERS

PRODUCERS

Below are some examples of decomposers and the habitat where they live. Choose one of these living things or another decomposer, and learn more about it. Using the internet and your school library, find information about the decomposer's diet. Determine which plants and animals the decomposer might break down. Using your decomposer, draw an energy pyramid showing the transfer of energy. Which plants and animals are a source of energy for the decomposer you picked? Do other decomposers receive energy by further breaking down detritus after your decomposer is done?

FOREST

Slug

DESERT

AQUATIC

Cleaner Shrimp

Termite

Drab Bonnet
Mushrooms

Arctic Lichen

GRASSLAND

TUNDRA

Quiz Based on what you have just read, try to answer the following questions correctly.

1 What is material left behind by plants and animals that have died called?

2 What are three types of detritivores?

3 What are housefly larvae called?

4 What makes up the largest group of fungi?

5 How many cells do bacteria have?

6 What type of decomposer is used to make some cheeses?

7 Are many types of decomposers endangered?

8 Is it safe for humans to eat morel mushrooms?

9 When did the United States issue a recovery plan for the American burying beetle?

10 What do scientists believe is the smallest known living thing?

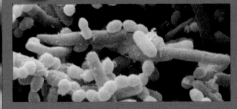

ANSWERS: 1. Detritus 2. Earthworms, maggots, and termites 3. Maggots 4. Ascomycetes 5. One 6. Mold 7. No 8. Yes 9. 1991 10. A type of bacteria

Key Words

antibiotic: a substance used to hold back the growth of very small living things, including harmful bacteria and fungi

consumers: animals that feed on plants or other animals

ecosystem: a community of living things and the environment where they live

endangered: at risk of becoming extinct, or no longer living any place on Earth

energy: the usable power living things receive from food that they use to grow, move, and stay healthy

enzymes: substances that help the process of decomposition

habitat: the environment in which an animal or a plant lives

matter: the substances all things are made up of

microscope: an instrument with a lens for making small things look larger

nutrients: substances that provide food for plants and animals

producers: living things, such as plants, that produce their own food

species: a group of the same kind of living things, whose members can produce young

Index

ascomycetes 15, 22

bacteria 6, 7, 8, 10, 11, 12, 14, 18, 19, 22
beetle 17, 18, 22

consumers 4, 5, 20

detritivore 6, 8, 9, 14, 22
detritus 6, 8, 9, 21, 22

earthworms 6, 7, 8, 14, 15, 22
energy 4, 6, 8, 20, 21

food chain 4, 5, 6, 8, 9, 20
fungi 6, 7, 12, 13, 15, 19, 22

maggots 6, 7, 14, 22
microbiologist 19
mildew 12, 13
millipedes 8, 14, 19
mold 4, 12, 15, 22
moss 16, 17
mushrooms 12, 13, 17, 21, 22

nematodes 16, 17

oil spill 18, 19

producers 4, 5, 20

termites 6, 14, 16, 17, 21, 22

woodlouse 6

Log on to www.av2books.com

AV² by Weigl brings you media enhanced books that support active learning. Go to www.av2books.com, and enter the special code found on page 2 of this book. You will gain access to enriched and enhanced content that supplements and complements this book. Content includes video, audio, weblinks, quizzes, a slide show, and activities.

AV² Online Navigation

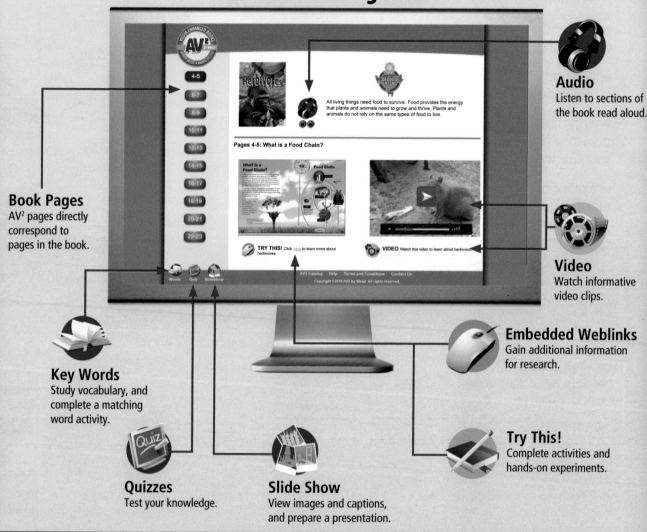

Book Pages
AV² pages directly correspond to pages in the book.

Audio
Listen to sections of the book read aloud.

Video
Watch informative video clips.

Key Words
Study vocabulary, and complete a matching word activity.

Embedded Weblinks
Gain additional information for research.

Try This!
Complete activities and hands-on experiments.

Quizzes
Test your knowledge.

Slide Show
View images and captions, and prepare a presentation.

AV² was built to bridge the gap between print and digital. We encourage you to tell us what you like and what you want to see in the future.

Sign up to be an AV² Ambassador at
www.av2books.com/ambassador.

Due to the dynamic nature of the Internet, some of the URLs and activities provided as part of AV² by Weigl may have changed or ceased to exist. AV² by Weigl accepts no responsibility for any such changes. All media enhanced books are regularly monitored to update addresses and sites in a timely manner. Contact AV² by Weigl at 1-866-649-3445 or av2books@weigl.com with any questions, comments, or feedback.